Jefferson went to work.

His room was small and stuffy. Horseflies buzzed around his head. They bit. The days were long and hot.

It took 18 days to write the paper.

It was only one page.

But Thomas Jefferson had written . . . the Declaration of Independence!

Meet THOMAS JEFFERSON

by Marvin Barrett

illustrated by Pat Fogarty

LANDMARK BOOKS®

RANDOM HOUSE 🏠 NEW YORK

RANDOM HOUSE and colophon are registered trademarks of Random House, Inc.

www.randomhouse.com/kids

Educators and librarians, for a variety of teaching tools, visit us at
www.randomhouse.com/teachers

Library of Congress Cataloging-in-Publication Data
Barrett, Marvin.
Meet Thomas Jefferson / written by Marvin Barrett ; illustrated by Pat Fogarty.
    p.   cm. — (Landmark books)
SUMMARY: An easy-to-read biography of the third president with emphasis on the
creation of the Declaration of Independence.
ISBN 978-0-375-81211-8
1. Jefferson, Thomas, 1743–1826—Juvenile literature.
2. Presidents—United States—Biography—Juvenile literature.
[1. Jefferson, Thomas, 1743–1826. 2. Presidents.] I. Fogarty, Pat, ill. II. Title.
III. Series. E332.79.B3 1989 973.4'6'0924—dc19 [B] [92] 88-19069

Printed in the United States of America

16 15 14 13

First Landmark Books® edition, 2001.

To Elizabeth, Irving, Mary Ellin, and Katherine

Contents

1

MEET
THOMAS JEFFERSON

Thomas Jefferson was the third president of the United States. And he was one of the most important Americans who ever lived.

Jefferson fought for his country. But he did not fight with a gun or a sword. He fought with words.

Thomas Jefferson wrote one of the most famous papers in the world. Many people think it is the greatest paper in the history of the United States. It is the Declaration of Independence.

Thomas Jefferson was born in Virginia on April 13, 1743. There was no United States of America then. Virginia was called a colony. It belonged to England. There were 13 colonies in America, ruled by the English king.

Virginia was the biggest colony. It went from the sea west to the mountains. The land near the sea was called the Tidewater. It was good farm land. Rich people lived there on great farms. These farms were called plantations.

West of the Tidewater, the land grew wilder. In the mountains lived many Indians. But the only white people there were a few hunters.

Thomas Jefferson was born in a house called Shadwell. It was on a farm between the Tidewater and the mountains.

Tom's father was named Peter. He was a farmer. Tom's mother, Jane, came from an old Virginia family named Randolph.

Sometimes Peter Jefferson went west into the mountains. There he visited his friends the Indians. He hunted and explored. He made the first complete map of Virginia.

Sometimes Peter rode east to the Tidewater. There he visited Jane's cousin, William Randolph. Mr. Randolph lived near the sea in a fine house called Tuckahoe.

2

TUCKAHOE

One summer morning when Tom was only two, the Jefferson family left Shadwell. Tom, his mother and father, and his three sisters were moving to Tuckahoe. Mr. Randolph had died. Tom's father had promised to care for the Randolph children.

Tom was too little to ride all by himself. He had to sit on a pillow in front of a grownup.

The family rode for three days. At last they came to Tuckahoe.

Tuckahoe was much grander than Shadwell. Ships from England tied up at docks nearby. In the ships were beautiful English chairs and fine English china for the house. The ships left filled with tobacco from the Tidewater plantations.

At the big house there were many slaves. Slaves were black men and women. They were brought from Africa to work on the plantations.

The slaves were bought and sold like animals. They had to do just what their owners told them. Some owners were cruel. Slavery was one thing Tom Jefferson never liked.

One thing Tom always liked was learning. At Tuckahoe the children had their own little schoolhouse. There they learned to read, write, and do arithmetic.

One of the Randolph children was a boy about Tom's age. His name was Tom too. The two Toms became good friends.

Near the schoolhouse was a pond. In the winter the boys skated on it. In the summer they swam in it.

The Jefferson family stayed at Tuckahoe for seven years. By then the Randolph children had grown old enough to care for themselves.

The Jeffersons packed their things. They said good-bye and headed home to Shadwell.

3

GROWING UP
AT SHADWELL

At Shadwell, Tom grew into a big, strong
boy. He had freckles and red hair. His
hands and feet were large. He was awk-
ward, but he was a good rider. He and
his friends often raced their horses. They
went swimming in the river. They went
hunting in the woods.

Tom's best friend was a boy named
Dabney Carr. Dabney's horse was fast.
Tom's was slow. But Tom bet that
Dabney could not beat him in a horse race
on February 30.

Dabney knew his horse could run faster than Tom's. He said he would be glad to race.

Days went by. February 28 came. Dabney thought he would be racing Tom just two days later.

But the next day was March 1.

All at once Dabney saw that Tom had played a trick. He could not beat Tom on February 30. There was no such day.

Tom had won his bet.

One night an Indian chief came to dinner at Shadwell. His name was Outasseté. Tom listened to his father and Outasseté talk. Tom liked the Indians. They were a proud and handsome people.

When Tom was only 14, his father died. Tom was now the head of the family. For a 14-year-old boy he was very rich. He owned a lot of land. He owned 30 slaves. He owned cows and pigs and horses.

Tom was going to a school near Shadwell. He could leave school now if he wanted to. He had no father to tell him what to do.

But Tom stayed in school. There he learned two more languages, Greek and Latin. And on his own, he learned to play the violin.

When Tom was 16, he decided to go to college. He packed his bags. He rode off to Williamsburg, which was then the capital of Virginia.

4

TOM GOES TO COLLEGE

Williamsburg was the biggest town Tom had ever seen. There were 300 houses. The main street was 100 feet wide. It was covered with sand and oyster shells. At one end of it stood the Capitol Building.

There, men from all over Virginia came to make laws. These men were called burgesses. And together they were called the House of Burgesses.

From the Capitol, Tom rode down the main street of Williamsburg. At the far end stood some low brick buildings. This was the College of William and Mary.

At William and Mary, Tom studied hard. Most of the other boys played cards and raced their horses. They kept slaves and spent their money on fine clothes. Tom had fun, but his studies came first.

One night one of Tom's teachers took him to the finest house in Williamsburg. It was the governor's house. The governor had come from England. He had been sent by the king to run Virginia.

The governor like young Thomas Jefferson. Tom came back often. He learned a lot from the governor and his friends. Tom knew that he could learn from people as well as from books.

One day a large band of Indians came to Williamsburg. Their chief was Peter Jefferson's old friend Outasseté. He was going to England to meet King George the Third.

That night Outasseté made a good-bye speech. There was a full moon. The Indians sat very still. Their chief's voice was strong and clear.

It was a night that Tom would remember all his life.

5

BECOMING A LAWYER

When Tom finished college, he decided to be a lawyer. In those days a man could become a lawyer in six weeks. Tom wanted to be the best lawyer in Virginia. He worked for five years.

He got up every morning at five o'clock. To wake himself up, he put his feet in cold water. At night he studied long past midnight. He felt a good lawyer should know other things besides law. So Tom studied history, science, and geography. He learned to read and write in four languages.

Tom did not work all the time. For fun

he played his violin. He danced with the
women in Williamsburg. He often went
riding. And there was good swimming in
a pond nearby.

Tom made many friends. One of his best
friends was a man named Patrick Henry.
Henry was poor. But he was a lawyer and

a burgess. He and Tom talked about many things. One thing they were worried about was taxes. They thought King George was making Americans pay too many taxes.

There were taxes on all kinds of things, like food and iron and rum. Every piece of paper a lawyer used had to have a tax stamp on it.

One day Henry stood up in the House of Burgesses. He spoke out against King George. He called the king a tyrant. A tyrant is a cruel ruler. He said other tyrants had been killed.

Many burgesses did not like what Henry said. They were afraid the king would be very angry. But Jefferson thought his friend was right. He too thought the king was a tyrant.

Henry's words were printed in the newspapers. They were read in all the colonies. Many other people thought Patrick Henry was right.

6

MONTICELLO

Jefferson became a lawyer in 1767. He was a country lawyer. He rode for miles through the hills around Shadwell. He helped many people. Many were poor. He never asked the poor people to pay him.

When he was 25, Tom Jefferson decided he wanted to be a burgess. He had many friends in the country around Shadwell. They all voted for him. He won the election.

He was one of the youngest men in the House of Burgesses.

Jefferson went to Williamsburg. There he met the other burgesses. One was a rich farmer and famous soldier named George Washington.

The burgesses sent a letter to the king. They wanted England to stop taxing America. They said that the colonies wanted to make their own laws and taxes.

King George told the governor to dissolve the House of Burgesses. This meant that new burgesses had to be elected.

The people elected the same men all over again.

Jefferson was very busy. He was still working as a lawyer. And he was building a new house.

Jefferson's new house would be on a hill near Shadwell. He called it Monticello. He wanted to make it the finest house in the colonies. He planned all sorts of new things for his house.

It would have doors that opened all by

themselves. There would be little elevators to carry food from one floor to the next. He drew up plans for a big clock to stand in the hall. It would run for seven days without winding. Also in the hall would be an arrow. It would show which way the wind blew outside.

One day a slave came to him with bad news. Shadwell had burned to the ground.

Now Jefferson worked harder than ever on Monticello. In a few months a small part of the house was done. Jefferson moved in.

Around the house he planted many flowers and fruit trees. There were apples, pears, figs, and nuts. Many of the things he grew had never been seen in Virginia before.

By now Jefferson was not working on Monticello just for himself. He had met a beautiful woman named Martha Skelton. He had fallen in love with her.

Jefferson was not the only one to fall in love with Martha. There were many other young men who wanted to marry her. For she was not only pretty. She was smart and lively.

Martha and Tom both loved music. One night they were playing together at

Martha's house. Other young men came
to call. The men stood on the doorstep.
They could hear the music coming from
inside.

The young men knew Jefferson had won
her. They went away.

7

A WIFE AND A WAR

Tom and Martha were married on New Year's Day, 1772. They went to live at Monticello.

In the fall Martha had a baby girl. She was called Patsy. The Jefferson family needed more room now. Tom and his men worked hard to finish Monticello.

The Jeffersons were very happy. But soon Tom had to leave home. He was needed in Williamsburg.

Virginia had a new governor. His name was Lord Dunmore. He did not like the

House of Burgesses at all. He dissolved the House again and again. But he could not keep the burgesses from meeting.

In March of 1773 the burgesses met in a place called the Raleigh Tavern. There they picked 11 men. One was Patrick Henry. And one was Thomas Jefferson.

These men were to write letters to the other colonies. They wanted to find out what other men were doing about the English laws and taxes. Many letters went back and forth. The colonies were drawing together against England.

In November of 1773 three ships from England came into the harbor of Boston, Massachusetts. They were loaded with tea.

On the night of December 16 some men dressed up as Indians. They went onto the ships. They dumped all the tea into the water.

They thought it was a good joke. They said it was a tea party for King George.

They called it the Boston Tea Party.
King George did not think it was funny.
He closed Boston Harbor. He said no more
ships could go there. He sent more soldiers
to America.

In March of 1775 Jefferson sat in a

church in Richmond, Virginia. His friend Patrick Henry was giving a speech. He was asking Americans to fight the king. "Give me liberty or give me death!" Henry cried.

News of his words raced like wind across the land. In all 13 colonies men shouted, "Liberty or death!"

In Massachusetts, farmers fired on English soldiers. Men on both sides were killed.

This was the beginning of a war between England and its colonies.

It was the American Revolution.

The leaders of the colonies met in the city of Philadelphia. They called the meeting the Continental Congress.

Jefferson set out for Philadelphia.

The Continental Congress had many problems. Most important was to find a general for the army. The Congress chose George Washington.

In the late summer Jefferson went home to Monticello. It was not a happy time. A baby daughter died. A few months later his mother died. And his wife was sick. Jefferson stayed as long as he could. But in May of 1776 he had to go back to Philadelphia.

8

THE DECLARATION OF INDEPENDENCE

All through the hot summer of 1776 Jefferson went to meetings of the Continental Congress. There were many things to do. They had to have a bigger army. They had to have a navy. And they had to raise the money to run them both.

The fighting had been going on for a year. The congressmen decided it was time to tell the world what the Americans were fighting for.

They chose five men to write down the reasons.

One of the men was John Adams. He later became a president of the United States. One was Benjamin Franklin. He was one of the most famous men in America. And one was Thomas Jefferson.

Jefferson was the youngest of the men. But the congressmen had all read papers he had written. They all agreed he was the best man for the job.

Jefferson went to work. His room was small and stuffy. Horseflies buzzed around

his head. They bit. The days were long and hot.

It took 18 days to write the paper.

It was only one page.

But Thomas Jefferson had written the Declaration of Independence.

The Declaration of Independence said that all men had certain rights. They had the right to be free. They had the right to choose their own rulers. If a ruler was bad, they had the right to choose another. Americans had decided that King George of England was a bad ruler.

The Declaration said the colonies were not English anymore. They were now the 13 "united States of America."

9

NEW LAWS
FOR A NEW STATE

The other men in Congress read the Declaration. They talked about it. They changed a few words. Then on July 4, 1776, they agreed to sign it. Copies were made. One copy was read to Washington's soldiers in Massachusetts. They cheered.

In Philadelphia a big crowd heard it read. They cheered too. All over America people rang bells. They shot off guns. They lit up the sky with fireworks.

In September, Jefferson rode home to Virginia.

The new governor of Virginia was an American. He was Patrick Henry. The burgesses were called delegates now. Jefferson took his seat in the House of Delegates in Williamsburg.

Virginia was no longer a colony. It was now the biggest and richest state in the new country. Jefferson hoped that if it made good laws the other states would copy them.

Washington was leading America in the war against the English king. Jefferson wanted to lead the fight against the old English laws.

Many of the laws were cruel. One said a woman could be burned as a witch. Another said a man could be hanged for stealing. Jefferson worked hard to change these laws.

Slaves were sent to Virginia on ships and then sold. Jefferson could not stop slavery. But he was able to stop the slave ships from coming to Virginia.

Another of his laws set up free schools for poor children. Still another was about religious freedom.

All Virginians had to pay money to the Church of England. Even the people who went to other churches had to pay. Jefferson wanted to stop this. But most delegates belonged to the Church of England. They did not pass his law.

To Jefferson the new country was like an empty notebook. He wanted to help put the right words in it.

In 1778 Martha had another baby. The Jeffersons called her Polly.

That same year the king of France sent soldiers to help the Americans fight the English.

The French soldiers were led by the Marquis de Lafayette. Lafayette was only 19. But he was already a general. He and Jefferson became great friends.

In 1779 Jefferson became governor of Virginia.

Virginia was lucky. Until now no battles had been fought there. Most of the fighting was in the North. Governor Jefferson sent soldiers north to help General Washington. He sent him food and money, guns and horses. Then, in 1781, English warships sailed up the rivers of Virginia. English soldiers landed. The Virginians tried to fight back. But there were not enough soldiers. Most of them were up north. The English pressed on into Virginia.

Soon Jefferson had to move the state capital west to Richmond. In a short time the capital was moved west again, to Charlottesville.

Jefferson stayed on at Monticello. One morning an American captain rode up the hill. He told Jefferson that English soldiers were coming to get him.

10

AMERICA
WINS THE WAR

The Jefferson family was having breakfast with some friends. The friends left.
Jefferson sent Martha and the girls away
in a carriage.

Soon a man ran to him. English soldiers
were climbing the hill! The man begged
Jefferson to go.

Jefferson let himself out by the back
door. He jumped on his horse. He galloped
down the hill.

He did not ride along the roads. He kept
to the woods. The English soldiers could

not find him. When night fell, he and his family were safe at a friend's house.

In October of 1781 there was a great battle at Yorktown, Virginia. Eight thousand English soldiers were trapped. On the sea behind them were French warships. On the land before them were American and French armies.

The American general was George Washington. The French general was the Marquis de Lafayette.

American and French cannon balls battered the English for two weeks. One night the English tried to get away in

boats. A bad storm came up. It drove the boats back to land. The next morning the English gave up.

Yorktown was the last big battle of the Revolution. The Americans had won the war.

Jefferson was not the governor of Virginia anymore. His two years as head of the state had been hard. He was glad that his country was no longer at war. Now he hoped he could live in peace at Monticello.

In 1782 Jefferson was elected a delegate again. But he would not leave home. He wanted to be with his family. Martha was very sick. All spring and summer he was at her bedside.

September 6, 1782, was the worst day of Jefferson's life. He wrote a few sad words in a book: "My dear wife died this day at 11:45 A.M."

11
NEW IDEAS FOR A NEW COUNTRY

When Martha died, Jefferson was heart-broken. He shut himself in his room. He did not eat or speak for days. For three long weeks little Patsy brought him food. She took care of him. She did all she could to cheer him up.

At last he came out. He saddled his favorite horse. He rode out alone across the hills.

His friends felt that he should go back to work. The Continental Congress was meeting. His friends asked him to go.

Once more he set off for Philadelphia.

In Congress no one could agree on anything. Everyone talked. No one listened. No one wanted to give any money to run the new country. They did not even know what kind of government they wanted.

America owned land west of the 13 states. Many congressmen wanted the states to divide this land up. It looked as though the 13 states might become 13 little countries.

Jefferson said that the western lands should become new states. The congressmen agreed with his plan. But they would not agree to keep slavery out of the new lands.

Jefferson also said that America needed its own money. He invented a new kind of money. It was made up of dollars worth 100 cents each. It was the simplest money in the world. Again Congress agreed.

In 1784 Congress asked him to go to France. France had been a good friend during the war. Both John Adams and Benjamin Franklin were there. Jefferson could help them make new friends for America in other countries in Europe.

He decided to leave Polly with an aunt and take Patsy with him.

12

FRANCE

On July 4, 1784, Jefferson and Patsy arrived in Boston. A ship called the *Ceres* was waiting there. They went on board. The next morning they were off to France.

Jefferson found that France was in trouble. The French king and the people in his government were very rich. But most of the people in the country were very poor. And the king was not helping them.

Jefferson went all over Europe. Everywhere he went, he looked for new things to send home. He sent plants and trees. He sent animals and birds. And he sent books. He sent 200 books to a young friend of his named James Madison.

Madison was in Virginia. He was working to get the delegates to pass the laws that Jefferson had written long before.

At last the delegates agreed to pass Jefferson's laws about religion. These laws did away with religious taxes. They said each person could worship God in his or her own way. The laws were called the Statute of Virginia for Religious Freedom.

Jefferson often wrote to another young friend. His name was James Monroe. He was working with James Madison on the Constitution of the United States. The Constitution set up a new government for America. Even though Jefferson was far away, they wanted his help.

Jefferson's French friends wanted his

help too. Many thought the new American government was the best in the world. Lafayette thought the French government should copy it.

On July 4, 1789, Jefferson gave a party. Lafayette was there. It was a happy night. They had worked out a new plan. It would give the French people many more rights.

But it was too late.

On July 14 thousands of people marched on the king's prison. They let the prisoners out. They cut off the prison keepers' heads.

Jefferson saw the people running through the city streets. He saw them throwing rocks at the king's soldiers. He saw them breaking into stores to get knives and swords.

A revolution had begun.

Jefferson had spent five years in France. Now he had to go back to America.

In September the Jeffersons were waiting for the ship to take them home. A man brought them news. The king and queen of France had been taken prisoner. The people of France said they were tyrants.

All wars are terrible. The French Revolution was one of the worst. Thousands of people were killed. And when it was over, France had a new tyrant. His name was Napoleon.

The Jeffersons were lucky they could leave France when they did.

13

AMERICANS CHOOSE SIDES

Two days before Christmas, 1789, Jefferson's coach rolled to a stop in front of Monticello. His slaves ran to him. Laughing and crying, they carried him into the house.

Not long after Christmas, a young man began to call at Monticello. He came to see Patsy. His name was Thomas Mann Randolph. He was the son of Jefferson's boyhood friend, Tom Randolph of Tuckahoe.

In February of 1790 Patsy married

Thomas. In March, Jefferson left home again. He went to the capital of America, which was then New York City.

George Washington was now the president of the United States. He had asked Jefferson to be secretary of state. Jefferson would take care of business with other countries.

Jefferson did many other things too. He ran the mint where the money was made. He ran the office where new inventions were brought.

Like these inventions, everything in the new country had to be tested. People did not always agree on the way things should be done.

The men who helped Washington run the country chose up sides. Some men followed Jefferson. They were called Democrat-Republicans. Other men were called Federalists. They were led by the secretary of the treasury, Alexander Hamilton.

Hamilton had been a poor boy. But his side was for the rich. It was for people in big cities. It was for people in the North.

Jefferson was rich. But his side was for the poor. He was the friend of farmers and people in the South and the West.

Both men worked very hard for their country. But they had many arguments.

Hamilton wanted the new capital of the country to be in the North. Jefferson wanted it farther south, on the Potomac River. The river divides Maryland and Virginia.

Jefferson won the argument.

Maryland and Virginia gave some land to the government. The new city would be named Washington, after the first president.

In 1796 Thomas Jefferson ran for president against Federalist John Adams. John Adams won. Jefferson became vice president.

President Adams signed many new laws. Jefferson felt many of them were very bad. One said that people from other countries had to wait 14 years to become Americans.

The worst laws kept people from speaking out against the American government. People from Europe could be sent back home. Americans could be sent to jail.

Jefferson could do nothing to help these people. Americans had fought a long war to win their rights. Now Jefferson was afraid these rights were being taken away.

There were many other Americans who agreed with Jefferson. In the 1800 election they voted against Adams. Thomas Jefferson was chosen as president of the United States.

John Adams was very angry. He left Washington without waiting to see Jefferson become president.

14

PRESIDENT JEFFERSON

On March 4, 1801, Jefferson set out from his room in the new city of Washington. He did not ride in a carriage. He walked. The path ran through a swamp. His shoes were covered with mud when he got to the Capitol Building.

There, Jefferson swore to uphold the laws of the country. He was now the third president of the United States.

Jefferson was not at all like the other two presidents. He did not like big parties. He did not like fancy clothes. People who

came to see him often found him playing
with his grandchildren on the floor.

Some people did not think that a
president should be so easygoing.

Once the English ambassador, a very
important man, came to call. Jefferson
met him wearing an old suit and slip-
pers. The ambassador was very angry. He

thought that the American president should dress up to meet him.

But most Americans thought that Jefferson was right. They liked his easy ways.

President Jefferson had bigger things to worry him. In the north of Africa there were a lot of pirates called the Barbary pirates. America was paying them to leave American ships alone. Now the pirates were asking for more money.

Jefferson grew angry. He moved fast. He did not send the money. He sent warships to fight the pirates.

Jefferson knew America had to fight. But he did not like wars. He thought the most important thing was learning. And there was still much to learn about America.

The West of America was still wild. Jefferson wanted to learn about it.

15

THE LOUISIANA PURCHASE

The United States went as far as the Mississippi River. No one knew much about the wild land beyond.

Jefferson's secretary was a man named Meriwether Lewis. Jefferson chose him to explore the Far West. Lewis called in an old friend named William Clark to go with him.

Jefferson told them he wanted to know about the mountains and the rivers in that part of America. He wanted to know about the Indians there. He wanted to know about the animals and birds and plants.

A year later, in 1804, Lewis and Clark set out.

France owned a huge part of the West. The French land lay between the Mississippi River and the Rocky Mountains. It was called Louisiana. The capital of Louisiana was the city of New Orleans.

New Orleans was very important to American farmers in the West. They sent cotton and other crops down the Mississippi River to New Orleans. There the crops were sold. Then ships carried them to cities in America and other countries.

The French could close up New Orleans at any time. Ships would not be able to come or go. American farmers would have nowhere to sell their crops. They would be ruined.

President Jefferson knew he had to do something. He sent his friend James Monroe to France. He told Monroe to try to buy New Orleans.

Napoleon, the head of the French government, said no. He would not sell New Orleans by itself. But he would sell all of Louisiana for 25 million dollars.

Monroe said America could not pay that much. The talks went on. At last Napoleon sold Louisiana for 15 million dollars.

Napoleon fought wars to get more land. Thousands of men died in his wars. With the Louisiana Purchase, Jefferson made America twice as big. And not one single person was killed.

16

PRESIDENT AGAIN

Things were going well for Thomas Jefferson as president. But he was worried about his family. Polly was very sick.

Polly was staying with her sister, Patsy. Jefferson decided to take her to Monticello.

There he spent as much time as he could with her. He read to her. He took her on rides around the garden. A slave pulled the little carriage along slowly so it would not bump too much.

But in April of 1804 Polly died. Her father was heartbroken.

Far away in Massachusetts, John Adams's wife heard the sad news. She wrote Jefferson a kind note. It was the first time he had heard from her since he became president. He wrote back. Soon he and the Adamses were friends again.

In the fall of 1804 Jefferson ran for president again. He was elected for another four years.

In 1805 the war with the Barbary pirates ended. America won. Never again would America pay the Barbary pirates to leave its ships alone.

A year later, Meriwether Lewis and William Clark came back from the West. They had gone all the way to the far Pacific Ocean.

It had been a hard trip. They had been gone so long that people thought they might be dead. But they had done what Jefferson had hoped they would do.

They brought back Indians with them.

They brought back maps of the rivers and
mountains. They had books filled with
notes about the animals and birds and
plants. They even brought back some live
grizzly bears. Jefferson kept the bears in
his garden in Washington.

In 1808 many Americans hoped
Jefferson would run for president again.
But he had worked for his country for 40
years. He wanted to go home to Monticello
for good.

17

THE UNIVERSITY OF VIRGINIA

Even at Monticello, Jefferson did not stop working. He was up early every morning. He rode, he farmed, and he studied. He read to his 12 grandchildren and played with them. He made them a fruit picker. It was a hook on the end of a long stick. There was a bag on it to catch the apples and cherries as they fell. Even a very small child could get fruit from the trees with it.

Thomas Jefferson was now called the sage of Monticello. A sage is a wise man.

He is almost always an old man who has lived a long and useful life. He has done and seen many things. He has been happy and sad. He knows what life is about.

People were always asking Thomas Jefferson for advice. He got more than 1,000 letters every year. His friend James Madison wrote to him. Madison was the fourth president of the United States. So did James Monroe, the fifth president. They still thought of Jefferson as their teacher.

The man who wrote most often was John Adams. They were the closest of friends until the day they died.

In 1820 Jefferson was 77. But he was busier than ever. Early most mornings he would ride four miles over to Charlottesville. There he was building a college. It was to be the University of Virginia.

Jefferson spent six years working on the university. His old friends President

Madison and President Monroe helped him. But he did most of the work himself.

He made plans of the buildings and the gardens. He told the builders how much brick and stone and wood was needed. He sent men all the way to Europe to find good teachers. He wanted the university to be the best in America.

Slowly the college buildings grew. Sometimes Jefferson could not go over to Charlottesville. Then he went out on his porch and watched the work through a telescope.

At last the college was finished. Jefferson made friends with many of the students. He would ask them up to Monticello for dinner.

There were always people coming to Monticello. It was like a hotel. There were 50 beds for people who wanted to stay for the night. One family stayed for ten months.

Everyone wanted to see Jefferson. Even people he did not know would come into his house. They would wait for hours just to see the great man walk down the hall to dinner. One lady broke a window with her umbrella to get a look at him.

Monticello cost a lot of money to run. Jefferson was not rich anymore. He sold his 7,000 books to Congress. They were the beginning of the great Library of Congress.

But this money did not last long. For a while it looked as if he would have to sell some of his land.

People all over the country heard of his troubles. They began to send money to help Jefferson.

18

THE LAST DAYS

One day a carriage rolled up to Monticello. Out stepped an old man. He moved slowly toward the house. Jefferson came out to meet him.

"Ah, Jefferson!" the visitor cried.

"Ah, Lafayette!" cried Jefferson. And they both burst into tears.

It was a happy visit. The two old friends had not seen each other for 36 years. They had many things to talk about.

They talked about the American and the French revolutions. They talked about all the people they had known. They talked of the past and the future. They were old men now. And they had each played a big part in the history of their countries.

July 4, 1826, was a big holiday in America. It was just 50 years since Thomas Jefferson had written the Declaration of Independence. Two of the most famous men who signed it were still alive. They were John Adams and Thomas Jefferson. John Adams was 91. Jefferson was 83.

At Monticello, Jefferson lay in bed. He knew he was dying. But he had fought to stay alive until this day.

It was a great day. All over the country guns were fired. Soldiers marched. Flags waved in the wind.

At Monticello it was quiet. Soon after noon, Thomas Jefferson died. Later on the same day, far away in Massachusetts, John Adams died.

It is hard to say what was most important in Jefferson's life. He did many things. He doubled the size of his country

without a war. He gave it many good laws. He was one of its greatest leaders. And he was a teacher to the presidents who followed him.

After Thomas Jefferson died, an old book was found in his desk. On one page was a drawing.

The drawing was of his tombstone. Jefferson had written the words he wanted on it.

Here was buried
Thomas Jefferson,
Author of the
Declaration of American
Independence,
of the Statute of Virginia
for religious freedom,
and Father of
the University of Virginia.

"By these," he had written, "I wish most to be remembered."

Relive history!

Turn the page for more great books . . .

Landmark Books® Grades 2 and Up

Landmark Books® Grades 4 and Up

Landmark Books® Grades 6 and Up

want to miss a thing. He could smell the lobster bait. Waves slapped against the hull as they chugged through the black water.

Dink watched the glow of morning color the horizon pale yellow. It made him remember the light he'd seen last night. Did the light have anything to do with the strange noises or the two green feathers?

The boat's gentle rocking made Dink feel sleepy. He closed his eyes. Then Walker was shaking him. Dink sat up and squinted into sunlight.

The waves rocked the boat back and forth. When Dink stood, he nearly lost his balance. "Where are we?" he asked.

"About five miles out," Walker said. "Wake up Ruth Rose and Josh, and we'll eat."

They sat in a patch of sunlight. Breakfast was peanut butter sandwiches and hot, milky cocoa from Walker's thermos.

Dink saw other boats in the distance. "Are those all lobster boats?"

Walker nodded. "Most of them are. A few fishing boats are out, too."

Josh looked over the side. "How do you catch the lobsters?" he asked.

Walker pointed to a machine. "That winch brings them up. I'll show you how it works."

Walker picked up a long pole with a hook on one end. He used it to grab the rope attached to a marker buoy. He snagged the rope onto the winch, pushed a button, and wet rope began whistling up out of the water. Fast!

A few seconds later a lobster pot surfaced on the other end of the rope. Wearing a rubber apron and gloves, Walker dragged it into the boat.

The wooden trap was covered with

seaweed. A few small crabs scampered out onto the deck. "Let's see what we've got," Walker said, dropping the crabs back into the sea.

Walker opened the pot's small door and reached in a gloved hand. He pulled out a wet, dark green lobster. The lobster waved its claws angrily.

"Those claws can break a finger," Walker warned. He snapped two thick rubber bands onto the lobster's front claws. Then he dropped the lobster into a tank of sea water.

"Josh, get the bait, will you?"

Josh dragged the heavy pail over. Walker pulled out a huge fish head.

"Oh, phew!" Josh said. "That's gross!"

"The lobsters don't mind," Walker said, dropping the fish head into the lobster pot. He fastened the door and shoved the trap back into the water.

"That's pretty much how it's done," Walker said, slapping water off his gloves.

"Can we pull another one?" Dink asked.

"Sure, and you guys can help. Grab some gloves out of that locker."

Ruth Rose brought out three pairs of

thick rubber gloves. Walker winched up another pot and held a wiggling lobster out to Josh.

"Hold him by the back so he can't reach you with his claws."

Josh held the lobster with both gloved hands. Ruth Rose and Dink snapped rubber bands onto the claws.

"Who wants to put bait in the pot?" Walker asked, grinning.

Dink volunteered while Josh faked gagging noises. Dink stuck his hand into the bait bucket, then dropped a bloody fish head into the lobster pot.

The morning grew warm, so the kids stripped off their sweatshirts. The ocean was calm. Sea gulls soared overhead, watching for scraps.

"Look, there's Rip," Walker said.

Rip pulled his boat up next to *Lady Luck*. When the boats were side by side, Rip tossed a line to Dink.

"How's it going?" Rip asked. He was wearing clean jeans and a T-shirt. He held a coffee mug in one hand.

"We got a few," Walker said. "My crew here was a big help."

"Are you going lobstering?" Josh asked.

Rip shook his head and flashed a grin. "Not today, kiddo. Just came out to check my buoys. Toss me the line, okay?"

Dink tossed his end of the rope toward the other boat. Rip caught it in his free hand. "Have a good day!" he yelled as he pulled away.

"Anyone want more cocoa?" Walker asked.

"I do," Josh said.

Dink turned around and saw something on *Lady Luck*'s deck.

It was a bright green feather.

Chapter 8

Dink snatched up the feather. Ruth Rose raised her eyebrows. Dink shrugged and stuck the feather in his pocket.

"Ready to head in?" Walker asked. "I promised Sis I'd get you back before lunch."

He started up the engine, and they chugged toward land.

Back at Walker's dock, the kids helped him hose fish goo and seaweed off the deck of his boat. Then he drove them to the castle.

"Sis's car is gone," Walker said. "She must be out doing errands. Will you kids be okay for a while?"

"I'm a little hungry," Josh said, grinning.

"Here, finish this." Walker handed Josh the bread, peanut butter, and knife. He waved and drove away.

"Where should we eat?" Josh asked.

"How about the playhouse?" Ruth Rose said. "I can wash those little dishes." She found a watering can next to the mud room door and filled it from the spigot.

On the way to the playhouse, Dink pulled the feathers out of his pocket. He told Josh how he'd found the third one on Walker's boat.

The kids studied the feathers, holding them up to the sunlight. "They're exactly alike," Josh said.

"Another parrot feather?" Ruth Rose

asked. "Where could they be coming from?"

Josh grinned. "From a parrot?"

"Very funny, Joshua!"

Dink suddenly remembered his dream. Screaming bats with green feathers...

Ruth Rose opened the playhouse door and they walked in.

"It's too cold in here," Josh said. "Why don't we eat out in the sun?"

Dink helped Josh carry the table out.

Ruth Rose brought out the dishes and set them in the grass.

"The rug looks pretty dusty," Dink said. "We should drag it outside and sweep it."

Josh was spreading peanut butter on bread at the table. "Can we eat first, then work? My stomach is talking to me."

On his knees, Dink began rolling up the rug. "Your stomach is—hey, guys, look!"

"Not another green feather, I hope," Josh muttered. He strolled over to see.

Dink pointed to a trapdoor in the floor.

"Yes!" Josh yelled. "I told you! The secret door to the secret dungeon!"

Ruth Rose ran over. "Let's open it!" she said.

The handle had a spring lock. Ruth Rose squeezed the spring, and the lock popped open. With all three of them pulling, they were able to raise the trapdoor. They heard a creepy whoosh, then cold, damp air escaped.

"Yuck, what a smell!" Josh said.

The kids stared into the musty-smelling hole. Stone steps led down to darkness. Even in the dim light, they saw footprints on the steps.

"Just like the prints we saw on the rug," Dink said.

They all jumped back as a hollow scream echoed out of the dark hole.

Chapter 9

"Something's down there!" Ruth Rose whispered.

Josh's eyes were huge. "Not some-*thing*," he whispered. "Some*one*. It's the ghost of Emory Scott!"

Dink put his hand in his pocket and felt the three green parrot feathers.

Taking a deep breath, he put a foot on the top step. "I'm going down," he said.

Dink walked down the steps, feeling along the cold stone walls. He tried not to think about slimy things that hung out in damp tunnels.

Then his hand touched something square and hard. A light switch! He flipped it up, and the space was suddenly flooded with light.

"It's a long tunnel!" he yelled.

Ruth Rose hurried down the steps. She turned to Josh. "Coming?"

"All right," Josh sighed. "But if anything touches me, I'm out of here!"

The tunnel was cold and narrow. They walked along the dirt floor. Small, cobweb-covered light bulbs hung from the ceiling. The air smelled rotten.

The tunnel went straight for a while, then turned a corner.

"Listen," Ruth Rose said. "I hear water."

"I hate this," Josh said. "I really do."

Dink turned the corner and found himself standing in water. Something let out a screech, and Dink froze.

Josh grabbed Dink around the neck.

"What the heck was that?" he squeaked.

"Josh, you're strangling me!" Dink croaked.

"Sorry," Josh said.

"Where are we?" Ruth Rose asked.

They were standing at the entrance to a cave. The rock walls oozed, and the floor was under water. Off to the left, another tunnel continued out of sight.

"I think I know where we are," Dink whispered.

"Me too," Josh said. "We're in the dungeon. I'd better not see any skeletons!"

"I think if we'd kept going through the cave yesterday," Dink continued, "we'd have ended up here."

"It's one long tunnel," Ruth Rose said. "From the playhouse to the ocean!"

Then something behind them made a loud squawk.

Josh jumped, nearly knocking Dink over.

"Look, guys," Ruth Rose said. "Over there!" She pointed to a dark mound up against one wall.

Dink walked over, splashing through the cold water.

"It's a tarp," he said.

Holding his breath, Dink grabbed one corner and yanked it away. Under the tarp were two cages, one on top of the other. Each cage held four large green parrots.

The birds panicked, beating their wings against the cage bars. Their screams echoed again and again off the cave walls.

"So much for the ghost of Emory Scott," Ruth Rose said.

Josh laughed. "Good! I don't know what I'd have done if I'd bumped into him!"

Dink pulled the feathers from his pocket. He held them next to one of the parrots.

"They're the same," he said.

"What the heck *is* this place?" Ruth Rose asked. "Who'd hide parrots in a cave?"

"I don't know," Dink said.

"Guys!" Ruth Rose said. She was looking down. "The tide must be coming in. The water is getting deeper!"

Dink and Josh looked down. The water was up to their ankles!

"The parrots!" Josh said.

The bottom cage was getting wet. The parrots shrieked at the rising water.

"Let's get them outside!" Dink said, grabbing the top cage. He lugged it into the dry tunnel.

Josh and Ruth Rose took the other cage. They hurried back along the tunnel with the parrots squawking in fear.

Dink stopped at the bottom of the stone steps and looked up. "Uh-oh."

"What?" Ruth Rose gasped.

"I thought we left the trapdoor open," Dink said.

"We did," Josh said.

"Well, it's closed now." Dink set his cage on the floor. He walked up the steps and pushed on the door. It didn't budge.

Josh climbed the steps, and they both shoved against the door.

"It's no use," Dink said. "The door must have fallen, and the lock snapped shut."

"What can we do?" Ruth Rose asked. "If the tide floods this tunnel..."

Dink walked back down the steps. "There's another way out. But we'll have to swim."

Chapter 10

"Where?" Ruth Rose asked.

"We can go back to the cave and swim out through the tunnel," Dink explained.

"But there are bats in there!"

"It's our only way out," Josh said.

The kids lugged the two cages back through the tunnel. The parrots screeched and beat their wings.

In the cave, the water was almost up to their knees, and rising.

"We better get out of here fast," Josh said.

Ruth Rose peered into the other tunnel. "I wonder how far it is to the beach," she said.

"It can't be that far," Dink said. "We're probably right under the castle."

"How are we gonna swim and carry these cages at the same time?" Josh asked. He glanced around the dark cave. "We need a raft or something."

"If the water's not too deep, we can walk out," Dink said.

He handed his cage to Ruth Rose, then stepped into the deeper water. It came up to his waist.

"It's kind of cold," he said, shivering, "but it's not very deep. We can carry the cages out."

"But what if it gets deeper?" Josh asked. "We can't carry the cages on our heads!"

"I have an idea," Ruth Rose said. "I read it in a Girl Scout magazine. It showed how to use your jeans as floats. You can make water wings by tying knots in the ankles and legs."

"You mean get undressed?" Josh said. "No way!"

"That's a great idea," Dink said. He climbed back out of the deep water, then kicked out of his sneakers and wet jeans. He tied knots in his jeans and put his sneakers back on.

Dink looked at Josh. "Come on," he said. "The water's getting deeper."

"Okay, but I feel weird," Josh muttered, pulling off his sneakers and jeans. The water reached just below his boxer shorts.

Dink tied knots in Josh's jeans, then dropped both pairs into the water. The air-filled jeans floated!

"Ready?" Dink said. They stepped into the water and balanced the two cages on top of the floating jeans.

"It works!" said Ruth Rose.

"This water's cold and yucky," Josh said.

"At least we can touch bottom," Dink said. "Okay, let's go."

The tunnel grew darker as they waded away from the cave. The water reached their chests, but got no higher.

The parrots were quiet, as if they knew they were being rescued.

"Do you think there are sharks in here?" Josh said. His voice echoed.

"No," Dink said. "Just a few man-eating lobsters."

Suddenly they heard a whispery sound in the darkness around them.

"What's that?" Ruth Rose asked.

"Calm down," Josh said, giggling. "It's just bats. We must've scared them."

"Are they friendly?" asked Ruth Rose.

"Not if you're an insect," Josh said.

Finally they saw daylight. Ahead was the ocean end of the tunnel.

"We did it, guys!" Dink said. They dragged the cages and soggy jeans to the beach near where they'd eaten their picnic.

"Boy, does the sun feel good!" Josh said, flopping down on the sand.

The kids rested and caught their

breath. Dink and Josh took the knots out of their jeans and spread them out to dry.

"I was thinking about these parrots," Josh said. "I have a book about endangered birds, and I think these guys are in it."

"Why would anyone hide endangered parrots in a cave?" Ruth Rose asked.

"Poachers," Josh said, pulling off his soaked sneakers. "Poachers catch rare animals and sell them for a lot of money."

"But who?"

Josh shrugged. "Someone who knows about the tunnel."

"I think I know who it is," Dink said.

Josh and Ruth Rose looked at him.

"Who?" Josh asked.

Dink looked sad. "Walker Wallace."

Chapter 11

"WHAT?" Ruth Rose yelled. "That's crazy!"

Dink shrugged. "I found one of the feathers in his Jeep and another on his boat."

Josh nodded slowly. "And when we had our picnic here yesterday, Wallis said Walker had been in the cave. Maybe he found the trapdoor in the playhouse."

"The footprints on the rug were big enough to be his," Dink said.

Ruth Rose stood up and wiped sand

off her wet jeans. "I don't believe you guys. Walker wouldn't break the law! And he sure wouldn't use his sister's house!"

"I hope not," Dink said. "Anyway, let's get the parrots up to the castle."

Dink and Josh tugged on their damp jeans and grabbed the cages. A few minutes later they burst into Wallis's kitchen.

She was writing at the table.

"We found out what's making those noises!" Dink blurted out.

The kids told Wallis about the tunnel to the cave and the parrots.

"A trapdoor in the playhouse!" Wallis exclaimed with wide eyes. "And a tunnel? How incredible!"

"It's like a secret passageway," Josh said. "Maybe pirates hid gold down there!"

"Well, I don't know about pirates,"

Wallis said. "But now I know how Emory Scott got all that marble and stuff up here!"

"What should we do with the parrots?" asked Ruth Rose.

"Show me," Wallis said.

They all trooped into the mud room. When the door opened, the parrots began flapping around in the cages. Their shrieks filled the room.

"Poor things," Wallis said. "Should we feed them? What do parrots eat?"

"Got any fruit?" Josh said. "That's what they'd eat in the rain forests."

Wallis went to the kitchen.

"I wonder where these guys came from," said Ruth Rose.

Josh studied the parrots. "Probably Africa or South America," he said.

"How would the poachers get them all the way to Maine?" Dink asked.

"By boat," Josh said. "Then a smaller

boat would bring them into the cave."

"A boat like Walk—"

Dink stopped talking as Wallis came back with two peeled bananas and a bunch of grapes. They dropped the fruit into the cages. The parrots grabbed the food in their beaks.

"They were starving!" Wallis said. She placed a bowl of water in each cage.

"I'm kind of hungry, too," Josh said. "We missed lunch."

"Well, we can't have that!" Wallis said. "Come into the kitchen."

While she made sandwiches, Dink explained about the light he'd seen in the woods the night before. "I bet there were more cages. They must take them out through the playhouse at night."

"We should hide down there and see who it is!" Ruth Rose said.

Wallis shook her head. "Absolutely

not. Those people could be dangerous!"

She brought out plates and napkins. "Today is Sunday, but tomorrow morning I'm going to call the state capitol. They must have someone who deals with poachers."

Wallis looked at the kids. "Promise me you'll stay out of that tunnel and cave."

Dink kicked Ruth Rose and Josh under the table.

"We promise," he said.

After lunch, the kids went back to the playhouse. They cleaned the dishes and swept the rug.

"I wish we could get these poacher guys," Dink said.

"I think we should sleep in the playhouse," Josh said. "Then if anyone comes, we'll grab them!"

"Josh, they'd grab *us* and stick us in

a cage," Ruth Rose said.

"Besides, Wallis would never let us stay down here," Dink said. "But I have another idea!"

At one-thirty in the morning, the kids were crouched by the window in Dink and Josh's dark room. They were fully dressed.

Josh yawned. "Maybe no one is coming tonight."

"Maybe they know we found the cages," Dink said. "Walker could've seen us from his boat."

"I still don't think it's Walker," Ruth Rose said. "But whoever it is will have to come to feed the parrots, right?"

"Right," Dink said. "Let's take turns watching. I'll go first. You guys can snooze."

"Wake me up if you see any bad guys!" Josh said, flopping on his bed.

"Well, I'm not tired," Ruth Rose said. "I hope they go to jail for a hundred years!"

She and Dink stared out into the darkness. The alarm clock counted away the minutes.

Josh began snoring.

"Look," Ruth Rose whispered a while later. "A firefly."

Dink saw a light moving slowly through the darkness. "Wake Josh," he told her. "That's no lightning bug!"

The kids tiptoed past Wallis's room, then hurried down the steps and out through the mud room door. Creeping silently, they approached the playhouse.

Moonlight fell on the clearing. A few yards from the playhouse, a dark car stood in the shadows.

Dink grabbed Josh and Ruth Rose and pointed. It was Walker's Jeep!

"I guess you were right," Ruth Rose whispered sadly.

The kids inched forward. Suddenly Dink saw a light coming from the playhouse.

A man was bent over, pulling open the trapdoor! A glowing flashlight lay on the floor next to his feet.

The man stood up. In the flashlight's beam, Dink recognized who it was.

Ruth Rose grabbed his arm. "Ripley Pearce!" she whispered.

A moment later, Rip disappeared down the steps into the tunnel.

Suddenly Josh bolted around the corner of the playhouse and through the open door.

Before Dink could say anything, Josh slammed the trapdoor shut. Dink heard the spring lock snap into place.

Chapter 12

"What's Operation Game Thief?" Dink asked the next day.

"It's an 800 number you can call in Maine to report poachers," Wallis explained. She brought more hot pancakes to the table.

No one had gotten much sleep. After locking the trapdoor, Dink, Josh, and Ruth Rose had run back to wake up Wallis. She'd called 911 and reported poachers on her property.

The police had come and arrested Rip. The officers gave Wallis the Operation Game Thief phone number.

Wallis had then driven Walker's Jeep to his house and brought him back to the castle.

"The Maine Fish and Game Department will have plenty of questions for Rip," Walker said. "Trading in endangered animals is a federal crime."

"How did Rip get the parrots?" Josh asked.

"He must have contacts in the countries where they were captured," Walker said. "The police will be checking his phone bills to see whom he called."

"He probably used his own lobster boat," Wallis said, shaking her head. "No wonder it always looked so clean."

"Why did he have your Jeep?" Josh asked.

Walker speared another pancake. "Rip's car conked out a few days ago, so I let him borrow mine."

"It was a perfect set-up," Wallis said. "Rip needed money, and he had contacts who would pay a lot for rare parrots."

"I wonder if he sold any other animals," Josh said, "like monkeys or snakes."

"We may find out yet," Walker said. He winked at Josh. "What made you decide to shut the trapdoor on Rip?"

"I got mad!" Josh said. "I wanted him to see how it felt to be in a cage."

"So that green feather on Josh's sneaker came from Rip, right?" Dink asked.

Walker nodded. "He probably brought it into the Jeep on his foot. And the one you found on my boat got there the same way."

Josh blushed. "For a while we thought you were the poacher," he told Walker.

"Well, *I* never did!" Ruth Rose said.

Walker grinned at Ruth Rose. "Thanks! What made you so sure?"

"You're too busy," she answered. "And you wouldn't be mean to parrots. You threw those little crabs back in the water yesterday."

"What will happen to the parrots?" Dink asked.

"I assume they'll go back to where they came from," Walker said. "And Rip will most likely go to jail."

"And thanks to you kids, I won't have to hear any more strange noises," Wallis said.

She grinned shyly. "But to tell the truth, I think I'll miss the ghost of Emory Scott. I kind of liked living in a haunted castle!"

Just then a loud screech came from the mud room.

Collect clues with Dink, Josh, and Ruth Rose in their next exciting adventure,

THE EMPTY ENVELOPE!

Josh watched a dark blue car pull away from the library as he, Dink, and Ruth Rose came down the front steps.

"Hey," Josh said, "wasn't that car parked outside Ruth Rose's house?"

Ruth Rose shrugged. "I don't know."

They hurried up Woody Street.

Suddenly Josh grabbed Dink and Ruth Rose. He yanked them down behind Miss Alubicky's front hedge.

"What's wrong?" Dink asked.

"Now that blue car is in front of *your* house," Josh said.

The kids looked at each other.

"That can only mean one thing," Dink said. "Someone's following us!"